Children Past and Present

by Matthew Frank

Table of Contents

Words to Think About

clothes

People wear many types of clothes.

future

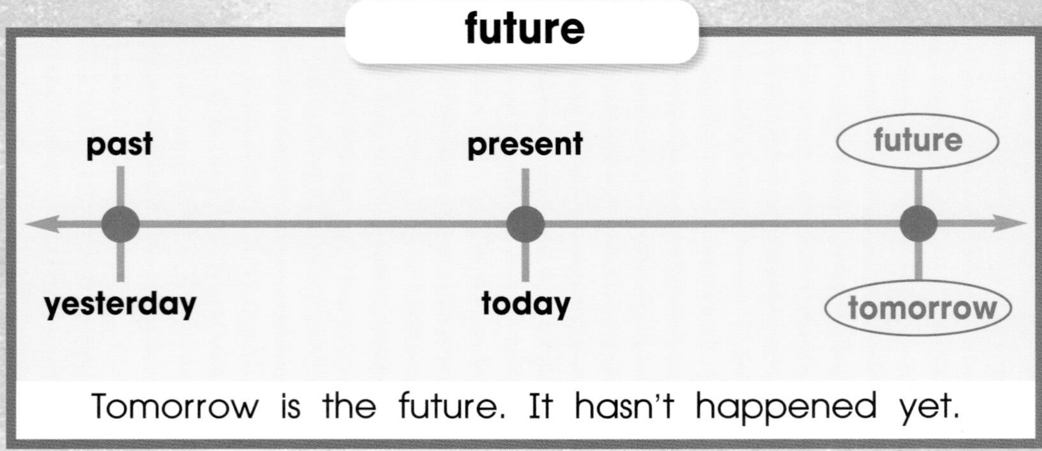

Tomorrow is the future. It hasn't happened yet.

past

These students went to school in the past.

Index

Glossary

circuit	(SER-kit) the pathway that electricity follows in an electrical device (page 3)
electromagnetic wave	(ih-lek-troh-mag-NEH-tik WAVE) a wave that has electrical and magnetic properties, such as a radio wave (page 23)
electron	(ih-LEK-trahn) a part of an atom with a negative charge (page 3)
filament	(FIH-luh-ment) the thin conductor in a lightbulb that glows when current passes through it (page 16)
generator	(JEH-nuh-ray-ter) a machine that converts other forms of energy into electricity (page 17)
Morse code	(MORS KODE) a code devised by Samuel F. B. Morse in which dots and dashes stand for letters (page 9)
Nobel Prize	(noh-BEL PRIZE) a prize established by Alfred Nobel for outstanding achievements in science, the arts, and the cause of peace (page 26)
phonograph	(FOH-nuh-graf) an electronic device that reproduced sound (page 11)
physics	(FIH-ziks) the branch of science that studies matter and energy (page 21)
receiver	(rih-SEE-ver) an electronic device that detects a signal (page 9)
transmit	(TRANS-mit) to send a signal (page 4)
transmitter	(trans-MIH-ter) an electronic device that sends a signal (page 9)
tuberculosis	(tuh-ber-kyuh-LOH-sis) a disease of the lungs caused by bacteria (page 8)

present

These students go to school in the present.

school

This school had one room.

tools

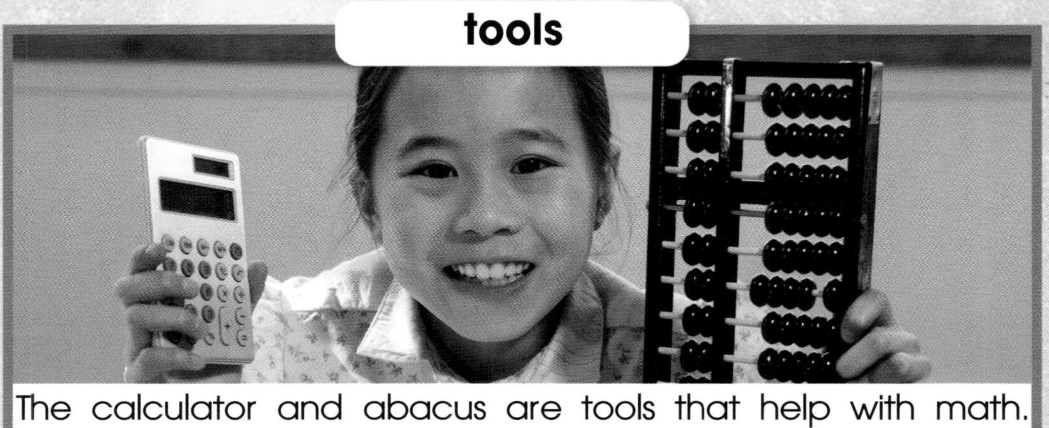

The calculator and abacus are tools that help with math.

Introduction

What would it have been like to be a child long ago? What games would you have played? What would **school** have been like?

How would your life have been different than it is today? How would it have been the same? This book compares children in the **past** and the **present**.

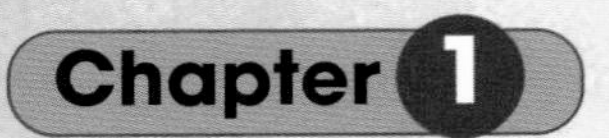

Chapter 1
Toys and Games

Children have always found ways to have fun. In the past, children played with dolls, balls, jump ropes, and other toys. They also played games and sports.

▲ Children enjoyed many toys and games in the past.

Today children still play games and sports. They still have toys, too. But now many toys use battery power. Many games use computer technology.

LOOK AT TEXT STRUCTURE

Compare and Contrast

The author uses the word "but" to compare toys in the present with toys long ago.

▲ Today children still enjoy many toys and games.

video game

skateboard

Chapter 2

Clothes

Hundreds of years ago, most children had only a few **clothes**. Their clothes were made at home. Later, families could shop in stores, but there weren't many choices.

▲ This girl made her own clothes.

Late 1800s

Girls wore dresses long ago. Little boys wore dresses, too!

Today families still shop for clothes in stores, but they also shop online. Children have many kinds of clothes—for play, school, and special times.

▲ **Today people can shop online and in stores.**

Chapter 3

Tools for Learning

Long ago, children had fewer **tools** for learning. They wrote on slates. They used quill pens. They rarely had their own books.

▲ These children used slates to share their answers.

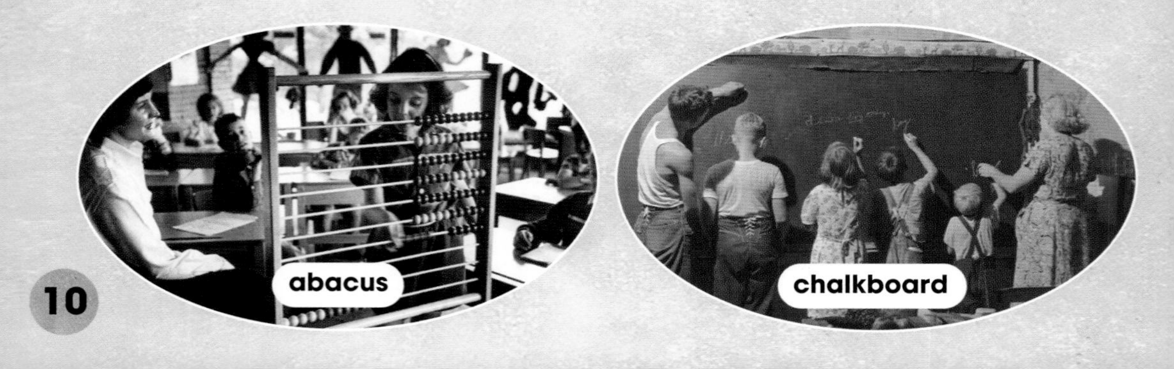

Today most children use books to learn. They also use computers. Computers help children communicate with others and find information.

▲ Many students use computers in school.

calculator

whiteboard

Chapter 4

Schools

In the past, not all children went to school. If they did, they often went to a one-room schoolhouse. Children of many different ages learned together.

▲ Students worked together and played together.

Today most children go to school. Some schools are big and others are small. Some children go to school at home.

▲ These students also work together and play together.

Conclusion

In some ways, your life would have been different if you were a child long ago. In other ways, your life would have been just the same.

Past

What do you think life will be like for children in the **future**?

Present

Glossary

clothes the things people wear to cover their bodies

See page 8.

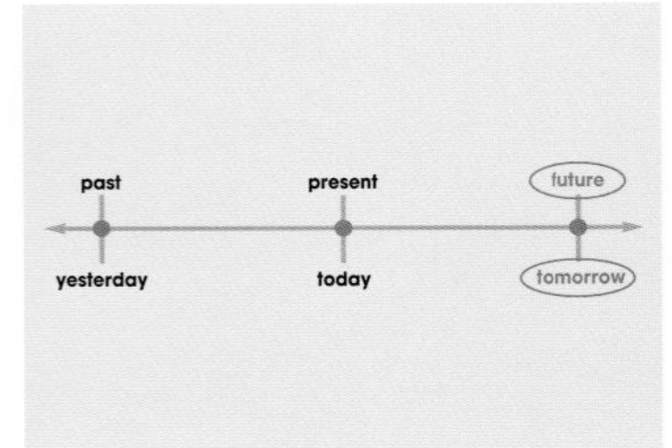

future time that has not yet happened

See page 15.

past time that has already happened

See page 5.

present time that is happening now

See page 5.

school a place where people learn

See page 4.

tools things that help people do work

See page 10.

Index